MW01538778

The Resiliency Skills Training Workbook
10-minute exercises to improve your health and happiness

Cover and interior design by Isaiah King Design, ikingdesign.com

This title may be purchased in bulk for educational or business purposes. For information, please email jessica@wellstudent.co

Printed in the United States of America

ISBN 9798624639270

First Printing March 2020

Well Student
https://wellstudent.co

The Resiliency Skills Training Workbook

10-MINUTE EXERCISES TO IMPROVE YOUR HEALTH AND HAPPINESS

Hello, and welcome to the Resiliency Skills Training (ReST) !

This workbook contains a careful selection of exercises and writing prompts that have been shown to build resilience, which in turn will strengthen relationships, deepen sense of meaning and purpose, and help you cope with stressors and challenges.

Table of Contents

How To Use This Workbook

There are many effective routes to achieving greater mental health and well-being and creating a fulfilling life. This workbook is intended to help you find what works best for *you*, and provide you with a broad repertoire of practices that you can integrate into your daily routine or turn to whenever you need them.

The workbook starts with a couple of foundational activities to set you up for success. The remainder of the workbook is divided into weeks, with 6 activities per week, followed by a reflection. If you like, you can go through the workbook sequentially and practice one new activity per day. Or, you may choose to focus exclusively on one activity, and practice it throughout the week, or anything in between. Remember, *the most effective activities are the ones that you actually do*, so please choose activities that match your needs and interests, and are appealing to you.

There are several ways to increase your chances of following through and completing the activities. You'll notice we ask a series of questions after each activity, about why you chose it, what obstacles you anticipate, and how you'll overcome them. These may feel a bit repetitive, but the more you mentally plan the exercise and how to address obstacles, the better your chances of following through, and the more benefit you'll get.[1,2] It also helps to establish a habit of wellness. You can help facilitate this by scheduling a consistent "wellness time" to use this workbook and plan your activities, such as every night before bed, or every Monday, Wednesday, Friday morning before breakfast.

This workbook is for you alone. While you are writing, do not worry about grammar, sentence structure, or even making sense. Try to write freely, without censoring your thoughts. There are a number of blank pages at the end of the workbook that you may use to repeat an exercise, make notes, or write about anything you like.

If you are interested in facilitating a group, which can provide increased support, connection and accountability, you may download a free facilitator's guide from my website *wellstudent.co*. This contains a curriculum for a 4-session group, as well as instructions on how to implement an online wellness program.

I hope you enjoy *The Resiliency Skills Training Workbook*!

Be well,
Jessica Gifford

Assess Your Progress!

Making progress in an area that's important to you can help reinforce the positive steps you took to make those changes. Is there a particular area that you'd like to assess your progress, from before to after completing the ReST Workbook? For example, you could measure changes in the following areas:

- Over the last 2 weeks on average, how would you rate your level of stress or overwhelm?

- Over the last 2 weeks on average, how satisfied are you feeling with your life?

- Over the last 2 weeks on average, how capable do you feel about handling challenges and meeting your goals?

1. What do you hope might change or improve over the next 4 weeks? Please write a question, or an area you'd like to assess here:

_____

_____

_____

Averaging over the last 2 weeks, please circle where you fall on a scale of 1-10 (with 1 being the lowest possible and 10 being the highest possible)

1   2   3   4   5   6   7   8   9   10

2. Is there another area you'd like to assess?

_____

_____

_____

Averaging over the last 2 weeks, please circle where you fall on a scale of 1-10 (with 1 being the lowest possible and 10 being the highest possible)

1   2   3   4   5   6   7   8   9   10

3. Is there a third area you'd like to assess?

_____

_____

_____

4. Averaging over the last 2 weeks, please circle where you fall on a scale of 1-10 (with 1 being the lowest possible and 10 being the highest possible)

1   2   3   4   5   6   7   8   9   10

Why it Works and What to Expect

The ReST Workbook is based on the simple premise that increasing your engagement in wellness-promoting activities will increase your well-being and capacity to thrive. The activities in this workbook have been selected because they have demonstrated effectiveness in:

- Improving physical and emotional health

- Strengthening relationships and social connection

- Reducing stress, anxiety and depression

- Increasing academic and work performance, productivity and goal achievement

- Managing stress and difficulty

Advances in neuroscience research have demonstrated that the brain is "plastic," or changeable throughout the lifespan. Your thoughts and actions influence brain chemistry and create neural pathways, which in turn affect your mood and behavior.[3,4,5] By engaging in the activities in this workbook, you are building neural pathways that promote health, happiness and resilience. Brain training, like all training, requires effort and repetition over time, until the neural pathways created by healthy activities and thought patterns, become well-established and habitual. Brain plasticity research proves that you have the power to change at any time--who you are today is not the same person you will be in the future.[3,4,5] The exercises in this workbook are designed to help you become your healthiest, happiest, most awesome self.

Engaging in the activities in this book is like a fitness program for your brain, helping it become stronger, healthier and more resilient. You may experience benefits immediately, or the effects may be subtle and occur over time. It may be helpful to remind yourself that, even if the results are not immediately noticeable, you are building new neural networks for positivity, and encourage yourself to keep going.[5] As with a new exercise routine, there can be some short term aches and pains for long term gains. Some of the exercises may stir up some difficult, uncomfortable or painful emotions. This is an important part of the process, and will pass in time. If you feel you need additional support at any time, please reach out to friends, meet with a therapist, or connect with other resources.

Think Big: Larger-than-self purpose

Reflecting on what is meaningful and important to you, beyond personal gain, helps you persist in working toward your goals, even when things get difficult. This exercise, based on research by Dr. Jennifer Crocker, starts out the workbook in order to help you stay connected to *why* you are working on wellness, and to help you maintain motivation through the full 4 weeks.

Benefits

Reflecting on the kind of impact you want to have on others or the world has been shown to:[6,7,8]

- Deepen sense of meaning and purpose

- Create greater calmness and well-being

- Decrease depression and anxiety

- Improve academic and work performance

- Strengthen social connections

- Increase persistence toward goals and through difficult tasks

Please write freely for 10-20 minutes in response to these prompts:

Purpose is not something you need to "find" or "discover" — it is something you can create anytime, and change whenever you want to. Please describe the kind of impact you hope to have on others, or on society in general, in the future.

_____

_____

_____

_____

_____

_____

_____

How will using this workbook and improving your well-being help you to become the kind of person you want to be, and have the kind of impact that you want to have?

_____

_____

_____

_____

_____

_____

_____

_____

_____

_____

_____

_____

_____

_____

_____

_____

_____

_____

_____

_____

_____

My motivation

There are always going to be times when your motivation fades—you're tired, busy, or not in the mood. The times when you most want to let self-care slip are often the times when you need it the most. Please create a 1-sentence personal motivation statement that captures *why* wellness is important to you, and what you hope to get out of finishing this workbook. It can be a condensed version of the Larger-Than-Self Purpose exercise, or anything else that you think will motivate you. You may read this statement daily, or to refer to it when your motivation is wobbling.

My motivational statement:

_____

_____

_____

WEEK 1

Week 1
Menu of Activities

Please look through the descriptions of activities 1 through 6 on the following pages, choose which one(s) you would like to do this week, and write them down. You may choose 1 activity to do multiple times this week, or choose multiple activities to do once each. To get the most benefit, aim to practice some kind of wellness activity at least 3 times this week, in addition to what you already do.

1. Set a Mini Goal

2. Emotional Skills: Noting Practice

3. Social Connection: Smile!

4. Health: Improve Your Sleep

5. Meaning: Spend Time in Nature

6. Self-Talk: Find a Positive Voice

7. Check-in

What activity/activities do you plan to do this week?

1. _____

2. _____

3. _____

When will you do them? Hint: adding goals to your calendar, or scheduling reminders, significantly improves your chances of following through.

1. _____

2. _____

3. _____

1
Set a Mini Goal

This activity involves setting a small goal that can be accomplished within half an hour or less, that you can do today, or within the week.

Use when

You feel overwhelmed, or want a sense of accomplishment and competence.

Benefits [1,2]

- Helps generate movement and momentum

- Reduces inertia, anxiety and depression

- Provides a sense of control and accomplishment

- Prioritizes what is important to you

Why it Works

Setting goals prioritizes what is important to you, generates action, and engages your pre-frontal cortex, all of which work to reduce anxiety and depression. Because mini-goals are small, they are easy to achieve, and build your sense of competence and control. Accomplishing a goal triggers a burst of dopamine, which generates positive emotion and reinforces forward momentum.[3]

Instructions

Please identify one thing that you would like to do today, or within the week, that can be completed in 30 minutes or less. If you have a larger goal in mind, break it down into small steps and choose one to work on. Ideas for mini-goals include:

- Making time for a self-care activity

- Completing an item on your To Do list

- Connecting with someone you've lost touch with

- Tackling a minor task you've been procrastinating

- Doing something fun

Please describe your mini-goal:

_____

_____

_____

_____

What made you choose this particular goal? How do you think completing it might benefit yourself and others?

_____

_____

_____

_____

When will you do it?_____

What might make it difficult to follow through on this goal?

_____

_____

_____

What can you do to overcome these obstacles?

_____

_____

_____

_____

Notes. After you've done your mini-goal, take a moment to reflect on how it feels to have completed it.

_____

_____

_____

_____

Is this a practice you'd like to continue? Why or why not?

_____

_____

_____

_____

2
Emotional Skills: Mindful Noting Practice

This practice narrating your thoughts and emotions, particularly during times of stress or distress.

Use when

- You have an "Oh #$%^&*!!!!" moment, or are in the throes of a stress response

- You experience painful or difficult emotions

- You have negative thoughts (self-criticism, judgment, hopelessness)

Benefits

- Improves mood, decreases anxiety and depression.[4,5]

- Speeds up recovery from stress, helps you handle conflict and crises more effectively, improves focus and productivity.[6]

Why it Works

Noting practice works by activating the prefrontal cortex and quieting the amygdala (where the fight or flight response takes place). Research has shown that *how you respond* to difficult thoughts and emotions has far greater impact on mood and well-being than the original thoughts and emotions themselves.[5,7,8] In other words, instead of trying to change how you think and feel about something, it is far more effective to change your "meta" response, or what you think and feel about what you're thinking and feeling.

Stressor or trigger – *can't change*

Primary response: what you think and feel in response to stressor

Secondary or "meta" response: what you think and feel about what you think and feel – work to accept, "note" and be compassionate about your primary response, rather than judging, suppressing, or trying to change it.

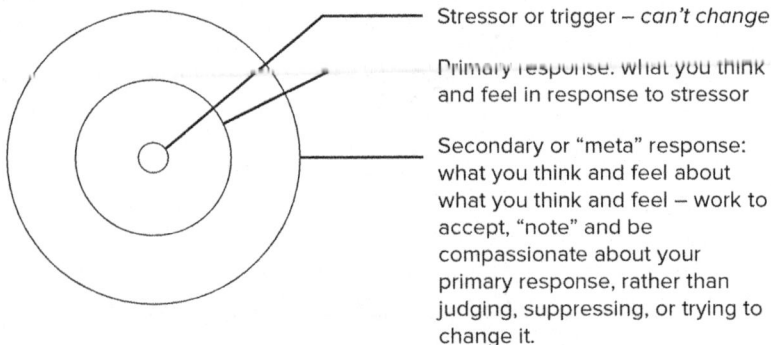

Instructions

Practice the following steps (NAN) several times throughout the day, or whenever you're experiencing difficult thoughts or emotions.

1. Notice: as soon as you notice you are having negative thoughts, or a negative emotional reaction, take a deep breath, and bring your attention to what you are thinking and feeling.

2. Accept: rather than ignoring, resisting or otherwise trying to change your thoughts and emotions, accept them.

3. Narrate: name whatever you are thinking and feeling, "noting" your experience to yourself, e.g. "You're feeling tense and angry and you're thinking this isn't fair." If it's helpful, you can imagine a compassionate observer in the role of narrator.

Take a moment to practice now. Please Notice, Accept and Narrate (NAN), in writing, what you are currently thinking and feeling.

_____

_____

_____

Please write a couple sentences about why you've chosen this activity. How do you think it might benefit yourself and others?

_____

_____

_____

What might make it difficult to practice Noticing, Accepting and Narrating (NAN) when you are in the grasp of difficult thoughts or emotions?

_____

_____

_____

_____

How can you overcome these obstacles and remember to practice NAN?

_____

_____

_____

_____

Notes. After you've practiced NAN a few times, please write what you've noticed. Was it hard or easy to practice? Did you notice any shift in mood, attitude, or actions?

_____

_____

_____

_____

Is this a practice you'd like to continue? Why or why not?

_____

_____

_____

_____

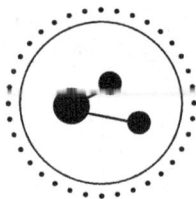

3
Social Connection: *Smile!*

This practice involves smiling, greeting, and conveying warmth and friendliness to the people you interact with.

Use When

You want to give yourself and others a mood boost, and improve social connection.

Benefits [9]

- Generates positive emotions in yourself and those around you

- Reduces stress

- Improves social connection (people who smile are thought to be more likable and friendly)

Why it Works

You smile more when you're in a good mood, but smiling can also give you a mood boost. It activates neuropeptides, which reduce stress, and triggers the release of the neurotransmitters dopamine, endorphins and serotonin, which give your mood a lift. Thanks to mirror neurons, smiling is contagious and boosts the mood of those around you as well. Smiling is also the universal sign of friendliness; when you smile you're viewed as more attractive, reliable, relaxed, likable and sincere. [9]

Instructions

Smile, nod and make eye contact with people as you walk by. Smile and greet people as you enter a room or conversation—focus on being happy to see them. Smile and practice conveying warmth and friendliness as you interact with others.

Please write a couple sentences about why you've chosen this activity. How do you think it might benefit yourself and others?

_____

_____

_____

_____

When will you do this? Please choose a specific day or days to practice.

_____

_____

Are there any obstacles that could get in the way of practicing smiling and conveying warmth?

_____

_____

_____

_____

What ideas do you have to overcome these obstacles?

_____

_____

_____

_____

Notes. After you've practiced this activity a few times, take a moment to write what you've noticed. How did you like this activity? Did you notice any shift in your mood, or how other people responded to you?

_____

_____

_____

_____

Is this a practice you'd like to continue? Why or why not?

_____

_____

_____

_____

4
Health: *Improve Your Sleep*

This activity involves engaging in one or two strategies to improve the quality and/or quantity of your sleep.

Use when

- You have difficulty falling asleep or staying asleep,

- You often feel tired, and want to sleep better

- You want to improve your health, mood, attention and performance

Benefits

Developing healthy sleep habits can have a dramatic impact on your well-being. Improving sleep: [10,11,12]

- Alleviates stress, depression, and anxiety

- Improves attention, memory, and academic performance

- Raises mood, motivation, optimism, energy and sociability

- Improves physical health: reduces cravings for food and substances, strengthens the immune system, accelerates recovery from injury and illness, and reduces risk for a number of chronic diseases

Why it Works

Sleep is essential to physical and emotional health. Poor sleep has been found to be a *cause*, as well as a symptom, of mental disorders. There are 5 stages of sleep, lasting 60-110 minutes each, that you need to cycle through several times a night for optimal benefit. Interruptions to the cycle cause you to start over. The first 4 stages are "quiet," increasingly deep sleep, the last of which produces physiological changes that help promote healing and boost the immune system. The fifth stage is REM sleep, where dreaming occurs. REM sleep enhances learning and memory, and contributes to emotional health. Sleep replenishes your physical, cognitive and emotional resources. One study found that sleep was the strongest predictor of mental resilience in repatriated prisoners of war.[13]

Instructions

Please choose one or two of the sleep strategies below to practice.

- Give your bedroom a sleep makeover. De-light the space, by covering all light sources, from windows to electronics, and/or wearing an eye mask to block out light. Reduce irregular sounds by using earplugs, a white noise machine, or reducing sound in the environment. Keep the temperature slightly cool at night. Treat yourself to comfortable sleepwear and pillows.

- Develop a sleep routine. Try to go to bed and get up at approximately the same time each day, even on weekends, and go through the same ritual each night, for example: brush teeth, get into pajamas, and read for 15 minutes.

- Unwind. If racing thoughts keep you up, try practicing a "mind dump" each night by jotting down your worries and unfinished tasks before going to bed. Alternatively, find an activity that helps you relax, such as crossword puzzles, meditation, or journaling.

- Avoid PM stimulants. Try to keep stimulants to the morning and early afternoon. This includes caffeine, nicotine, vigorous exercise, bright light, and adrenaline-inducing shows.

- Regulate your biological clock. Get outside in the morning for some daylight. If you can't do that, expose yourself to bright light in the morning, and dim, yellow-toned light in the evening.

Please write a couple sentences about why you've chosen this activity. How do you think it might benefit yourself and others?

_____

_____

_____

Which sleep strategies will you try, and when will you do them?

_____

_____

Are there any obstacles that could get in the way of practicing good sleep habits?

_____

_____

_____

How will you overcome these obstacles?

_____

_____

_____

Notes. After you've worked on improving your sleep habits, take a moment to write what you've noticed. How easy or hard was it to implement this activity? Did you notice any improvement in the quality or quantity of your sleep? What impact did it have on your mood, energy, focus, interactions, etc?

_____

_____

_____

Is this a practice you'd like to continue? Why or why not?

_____

_____

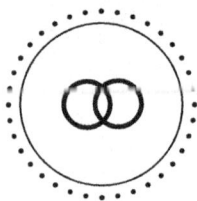

5
Meaning: Spend Time in Nature

This strategy involves spending time outdoors, in a natural setting.

Use when

You feel stressed, mentally cluttered or drained, or anytime you want to unwind and recharge.

Benefits

Spending time in nature: [14,15,16,17]

- Helps you connect to something larger than yourself

- Improves attention and restores mental energy,

- Relieves stress

- Reduces depression, anxiety and ADHD symptoms

- Boosts the immune system

Why it works

Nature works primarily by lowering stress. Physiological measurements of stress hormones, respiration, heart rate, and sweating indicate that even a short amount of time outdoors is calming and sharpens performance.[14] A study in Japan found that a 15-minute walk in the woods led to a 16% decrease in the stress hormone cortisol, a 2% drop in blood pressure, and a 4% drop in heart rate.[18] Even a view of nature, or looking at pictures of natural landscapes, has a positive effect. People with a window view of trees and grass have been shown to recover faster in hospitals, perform better in school, and display less violent behavior.[14,19]

Instructions

Get outside and spend 20+ minutes in a natural setting. Leave your phone behind, and really take in your surroundings. Spend a minute or two paying attention to each of your senses.

Please write a couple sentences about why you've chosen this activity. How do you think it might benefit yourself and others?

_____

_____

_____

When will you do it?

_____

What obstacles might come up to make it difficult to get outside?

_____

_____

_____

How will you overcome these obstacles?

_____

_____

_____

Notes. After you've spent some time in nature, please take a moment to reflect on what you noticed. Did it have an impact on your mood, attitude, or actions?

_____

_____

_____

Is this a practice you'd like to continue? Why or why not?

_____

_____

6
Self-Talk: Find a Positive Voice

This activity involves identifying a kind, compassionate perspective or voice, in order to shift from negative to more positive self-talk.

Use When

You want to engage in self-talk that lifts you up and helps you become your best self.

Benefits

Positive self-talk:[7,8]

- Improves mood and well-being

- Promotes positive self-image

- Helps you achieve your goals

- Enhances performance

Why it Works

Self-talk reflects the stories you tell yourself about who you are, and how you should, or shouldn't, behave. It serves to explain or make sense of other people, events, and the world. How you make meaning out of what happens in your life dictates your emotional response, and often influences your actions.[20] Learning to talk to yourself in ways that are supportive and encouraging, rather than critical or demeaning, has an enormous impact on your well-being and your personal and professional success.[8] This practice, of identifying the source of a positive voice outside of yourself, side-steps your own perspective on yourself, which can be slow to change.

Instructions

Please take a few moments to reflect on a positive, supportive, compassionate and encouraging voice for yourself. This could be:

- A friend, relative or mentor who consistently sees the best in you

- A real life inspirational figure whom you respect and admire, whether alive or deceased

- An imaginary or mythical figure, such as a spirit guide, a superhero, or the character of a book or movie

Please describe the owner of the positive voice in as much detail as you can. Who are they? What are they like?

_____

_____

_____

_____

What is it about this person (or being) that makes you trust them to be supportive, caring, and to always have your best interests at heart?

_____

_____

_____

Over the next few days, practice bringing this voice to mind whenever you feel stressed, down on yourself, or are struggling with something, and think about what they would tell you in this situation.

Please write a couple sentences about why you've chosen this activity. How do you think it might benefit yourself and others?

_____

_____

_____

_____

How will you remember to access this positive voice when you need it the most?

What obstacles might come up to make it difficult to access this positive voice?

_____

_____

_____

_____

What can you do to overcome these obstacles?

_____

_____

_____

_____

When you've practiced using this positive voice a few times, please take a moment to reflect on what you've noticed. How does it feel to talk to yourself in this way? What impact has it had on your mood, how you see yourself, and how you respond to difficulty?

_____

_____

_____

_____

Is this a practice you'd like to continue? Why or why not?

_____

_____

_____

_____

7
Check-in

Congratulations on completing the first week of your
ReST Workbook! Please take a moment to check-in with yourself about
how you're doing, what you've learned, and
where you want to go from here.

How are you doing right now?

_____

_____

_____

_____

What have you noticed from week 1? Please describe what you've
learned, any progress you've made, or any changes you've noticed
over the course of the week.

_____

_____

_____

_____

What you would like to remember, or remind yourself of, in the
upcoming week?

_____

_____

_____

WEEK 2

Week 2
Menu of Activities

Please look through the activities, choose which one(s) you would like to do this week, and write them down. You may choose 1 activity to do multiple times this week, or choose multiple activities to do once each. To get the most benefit, aim to practice some kind of wellness activity at least 3 times this week, in addition to what you already do.

1. Set a Mini Goal

2. Emotional Skills: What Went Well, and Why

3. Social Connection: Acts of Kindness

4. Health: Exercise

5. Meaning: Explore Your Values

6. Self-Talk: Write Yourself a Letter

7. Check-in

What activity/activities do you plan to do this week?

1. _____

2. _____

3. _____

When will you do them?

1. _____

2. _____

3. _____

1
Set a Mini Goal

This activity involves setting a small goal that can be accomplished within half an hour or less, that you can do today, or within the week.

Use when

You feel overwhelmed, or want a sense of accomplishment and competence.

Benefits [1,2]

- Helps generate movement and momentum

- Reduces inertia, anxiety and depression

- Provides a sense of control and accomplishment

- Prioritizes what is important to you

Why it Works

Setting goals prioritizes what is important to you, generates action, and engages your pre-frontal cortex, all of which work to reduce anxiety and depression. Because mini-goals are small, they are easy to achieve, and build your sense of competence and control. Accomplishing a goal triggers a burst of dopamine, which generates positive emotion and reinforces forward momentum.[3]

Instructions

Please identify one thing that you would like to do today, or within the week, that can be completed in 30 minutes or less. If you have a larger goal in mind, break it down into small steps and choose one to work on. Ideas for mini-goals include:

- Making time for a self-care activity

- Completing an item on your To Do list

- Connecting with someone you've lost touch with

- Tackling a minor task you've been procrastinating

- Doing something fun

Please describe your mini-goal:

_____

_____

_____

_____

What made you choose this particular goal? How do you think completing it might benefit yourself and others?

_____

_____

_____

_____

When will you do it?_____

What might make it difficult to follow through on your mini goal?

_____

_____

_____

_____

What can you do to overcome these obstacles?

_____

_____

_____

_____

_____

Notes. After you've done your mini-goal, take a moment to reflect on how it feels to have completed it.

_____

_____

_____

_____

_____

Is this a practice you'd like to continue? Why or why not?

_____

_____

_____

_____

_____

2
Emotional Skills: *What Went Well and Why?*

This practice, developed by Dr. Martin Seligman, involves
spending a few minutes reflecting on what went well during
the day, and why it went well.

Use When

You want to improve your mood, increase your sense of agency, and
train your mind to notice the positive.

Benefits

This practice has been shown to:[4-7]

- Improve physical health and reduce aches and pains

- Increase happiness and reduce depression

- Improve sleep

- Help you recognize the role *you* play in things going well

- Improve relationships, and academic and professional success

Why it Works

Reflecting on what went well works by bringing the positive things that
are happening in your life into focus, countering the natural human
tendency to zero in on what went wrong, or what you're anxious about.
Practicing this exercise corrects this negative skew, and helps reduce
stress, anxiety, and depression and generate feelings of gratitude, calm
and confidence. Over time, you will start to automatically seek out the
good, creating an upward spiral of positive emotion.[4-7]

Instructions

Please spend a few minutes at the end of the day reflecting on what went well during the day. Please take a few minutes to write in detail about 1-3 things that went well:

_____

_____

_____

Now, please write why each thing went well. What did you do, or others do, to contribute to it going well? Were there resources or circumstances that worked in your favor?

_____

_____

_____

_____

Please write a couple sentences about why you've chosen this activity. How do you think it might benefit you and others?

_____

_____

_____

_____

Is this something you'd like to practice on a more regular basis? Why or why not?

If yes, what might get in the way?

_____

_____

_____

_____

How will you overcome these obstacles?

_____

_____

_____

_____

_____

Notes. After you've practiced this a few times, please take a moment to reflect on what you've noticed. What impact do you think this practice has had on your mood, attitude, or actions?

_____

_____

_____

_____

_____

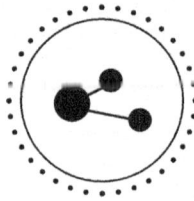

3
Social Connection: Acts of Kindness

This strategy involves engaging in small acts of
kindness or generosity.

Use when
You want to lift other people's spirits, as well as your own.

Benefits
This exercise will help you to:[7-10]

- Increase happiness over the course of the week, and even a month later

- Strengthen social engagement and connection

- See yourself in a positive light, as having something to contribute

Why it Works
Acts of genuine kindness or altruism raise our own levels of hope, joy
and happiness, and act as a buffer against stress and depression.[10]
Altruism:

- Raises levels of oxytocin, which has been referred to as the "love"
  or "bonding" hormone, as it fosters connection, boosts positive
  emotion, and relieves stress.[11]

- Gets you out of your own head and focused on others.[7]

- Strengthens social bonds. Kindness generates appreciation,
  goodwill and reciprocity, which brings people closer together.[7,9,10]

- Changes how you see yourself. By acting with generosity, you begin to see yourself as a kind, generous and helpful person.[7]

Instructions

- Choose a "Kindness Day" to engage in 3-5 acts of kindness.

- You may choose to be kind to strangers (e.g. paying an expired parking meter, leaving nice notes in random places), or friends (e.g. giving a stellar compliment, making dinner)

- For the most impact, vary what you do rather than performing the same kindness multiple times

- For this exercise to be effective it is essential that the kindness is offered freely, not out of a sense of obligation

What day would you like to be your Kindness Day?

_____

Please write a couple sentences about why you've chosen this activity. How do you think it might benefit you and others?

_____

_____

_____

_____

What obstacles might get in the way of performing acts of kindness?

_____

_____

_____

What can you do to overcome these obstacles?

_____

_____

_____

_____

After your Kindness Day, please take a moment to reflect on how it went. How did it feel to do this practice? What impact did it have on your mood? How did your kindness recipients respond?

_____

_____

_____

_____

_____

Is this a practice you'd like to continue? Why or why not?

_____

_____

_____

_____

_____

4
Health: *Exercise*

This practice involves engaging in a few additional
minutes of exercise a day.

Use When

You want to increase your energy and improve your physical and
emotional health.

Benefits

Regular physical exercise has been shown to:[12-16]

- Reduce stress, anxiety and depression (as effectively as
antidepressant medication!)

- Promote better sleep and boost energy

- Improve attention, memory, and performance

- Help maintain weight and promote positive body image

- Prevent a wide range of health issues, including heart disease,
stroke, diabetes, arthritis, depression, and Alzheimer's

- Extend lifespan

Why it Works

Our bodies were designed for physical activity and movement.[12,13,16] Up
until the age of industrialization only 200 years ago, people were
physically active from dawn to dusk. Exercise increases blood flow,
delivering "fuel" to the brain, muscles and organs, improving physical

and mental health and cognitive performance. Exercise also regulates the release of the neurotransmitters serotonin, dopamine & noropinophrine, all of which are associated with positive mental health [12,14]

Instructions

If you do not enjoy the gym, staying active in other ways can have an even greater impact on health and well-being than work-outs.[13,16] It is essential to pick an activity that you will *enjoy,* and that will fit your schedule and lifestyle. Please choose from the list below, or any other physical activity that appeals to you, and try it out for at least 3 days this week.

- Start the day with 5 minutes of cardiovascular exercise. A solo dance party is a great way to start the day! As little as 5-minutes of aerobic exercise a day has been shown to improve health and increased life span.[15]

- Go for a 15-minute walk after meals. Moving after eating dramatically reduces the post-meal blood sugar spikes that can wreak havoc on your health and mood.[13]

- Take a 5-minute break from work/study every 90 minutes to move around. In addition to increasing your activity level, this will replenish your energy, and refresh your ability to focus, increasing efficiency.[12]

- Reduce sitting time by any means possible.[13]

- Make it social. Invite a friend on a walk, or to sign up for an exercise class with you. This will help you be accountable to someone else, and make it more fun.

Making a small, realistic change is generally more successful and sustainable than more ambitious goals.

What would you like to do to increase your physical activity this week?

_____

When would you like to do it?

_____

Please write a couple sentences about why you've chosen this activity. How do you think it might benefit you and others?

_____

_____

_____

_____

What obstacles might get in the way of you exercising or becoming more active?

_____

_____

_____

How will you overcome these obstacles?

_____

_____

_____

_____

After engaging in more physical activity for a couple of days, please take a moment to reflect on how it is going. What impact do you think it has had on how you're feeling physically and emotionally?

_____

_____

_____

_____

Is this a practice you'd like to continue? Why or why not?

_____

_____

_____

5
Meaning: Explore Your Values

This exercise involves reflecting on the values that are most important to you, and how you can express them in daily life.

Use When

You want to feel calmer and more confident, improve your overall well-being, connect to what's important to you, or need help making a decision or choosing a direction.

Benefits

This exercise has been shown to:[2,11,17,18,19]

- Improve mental and physical health

- Boost Grade Point Average and increase work satisfaction, engagement and effectiveness

- Make people feel more confident, in control, and capable of dealing with stress

- Increase sense of connection and empathy

- Strengthen motivation and follow-through on personal goals

- Help people reduce substance use

Why it Works

Reflecting on your values works by tapping into a powerful source of motivation: it connects you to what you care about most, and reminds you of the kind of person you want to be. Writing about your values helps you recognize and capitalize on your own strengths and create a positive narrative about yourself. It makes you more likely to believe you can improve difficult or stressful situations through effort, and makes you more proactive. [2,11,17,18,19]

Instructions

Step 1: Please take a moment to reflect on what is most important to you. Choose 3 values that feel most important to you right now, either from the list below, or you may add your own. You may pick values that are existing strengths, or ones that you aspire to and would like to develop in yourself.

What 3 values feel most important to you in your life right now?

1._____2._____3._____

Accountability	Genuineness	Quality over quantity
Abundance	Good will	Reciprocity
Accuracy	Goodness	Recognition
Achievement	Gratitude	Relaxation
Adventure	Hard work	Reliability
Authenticity	Harmony	Resourcefulness
Autonomy	Healing	Respect for others
Balance	Healthy	Responsibility
Beauty	Holistic Living	Responsiveness
Caring	Honesty	Results
Challenge	Honor	Romance
Change	Improvement	Sacrifice
Clarity	Independence	Safety
Cleanliness/Orderliness	Individuality	Satisfying others
Collaboration	Initiative	Security
Commitment	Inner peace	Self-awareness
Communication	Innovation	Self-confidence
Community	Integrity	Self-esteem
Compassion	Intelligence	Self-expression
Competence	Intensity	Self-improvement
Confidence	Intimacy	Self-love

Connection	Intuition	Self-reliance
Conservation	Joy	Self-trust
Cooperation	Justice	Sensuality
Courage	Knowledge	Service
Creativity	Leadership	Simplicity
Credibility	Learning	Sincerity
Decisiveness	Love	Skill
Democracy	Loyalty	Solitude
Determination	Meaning	Speed
Discipline	Merit	Spirituality
Discovery	Moderation	Stability
Diversity	Modesty	Status/Recognition
Education	Nature	Straightforwardness
Efficiency	Nurturing	Strength
Environment	Open-mindedness	Success
Equality	Openness	Systemization
Excellence	Optimism	Teamwork
Exploration	Patriotism	Timeliness
Fairness	Peace/Non-violence	Tradition
Faith	Perseverance	Tranquility
Faithfulness	Personal growth	Trust
Family	Pleasure	Trustworthiness
Flair	Power/Influence	Truth
Flexibility	Practicality	Unity
Forgiveness	Preservation	Variety
Freedom	Problem-solving	Vitality
Friendship	Professionalism	Vulnerability
Frugality	Progress	Wealth
Fulfillment	Prosperity	Wisdom
Fun	Punctuality	
Generosity	Purpose	

Step 2: Now, please choose one of your top 3 values and write freely for 10-15 minutes about why this value is important to you.

_____

_____

_____

_____

_____

_____

_____

_____

_____

_____

_____

_____

_____

_____

_____

_____

_____

_____

_____

_____

_____

_____

_____

_____

_____

Step 3: How do you express this value in your daily life, including what you did today? How would you like to express this value in the future?

_____

_____

_____

_____

_____

_____

_____

_____

_____

_____

_____

_____

_____

_____

_____

_____

_____

_____

_____

_____

_____

_____

_____

We often get caught up in the day-to-day, and our values fade into the background. What ideas do you have to remind yourself of what is important to you, to keep your values in the foreground? (This could mean placing an image, word, or quote in a visible location, wearing a bracelet, changing your screensaver, etc)

_____

_____

_____

_____

What might get in the way of you staying connected to your values?

_____

_____

_____

_____

What can you do to overcome these obstacles?

_____

_____

_____

_____

How did it feel to take time to reflect on your values?

_____

_____

_____

_____

Is this a practice you'd like to do again in the future? Why or why not?

_____

_____

6
Self-Talk: *Write Yourself a Letter*

This practice, based on the work of Dr. Kristen Neff, involves involves writing yourself a letter, and offering yourself support, kindness, and compassion, about a specific situation that is causing you stress or suffering.

More exercises by Dr. Neff can be found at www.self-compassion.org

Use When

You are experiencing difficult or painful emotions (stress, anger, self-judgement, insecurity, etc.) related to a specific situation.

Benefits

This exercise helps you develop a more compassionate stance toward yourself, which will:[20,21]

- Improve mood, reduce depression and anxiety

- Build confidence and positive self-image

- Increase persistence through challenges and achievement of goals

- Help you bounce back from setbacks and difficulties

- Reduce isolation and remind you that you are not alone in your struggles

Why it Works

This practice, especially if done regularly, helps tame the voices of self-doubt, self-criticism and judgement. These negative thought patterns have been shown to be major contributors to depression and anxiety.[20,22] Many people think that self-criticism will motivate them to do better in the future, but the opposite is true. People who are self-compassionate are more willing to challenge themselves and take the risks necessary to pursue important goals.[20,21] This exercise helps to generate a sense of self-worth that is not tied to performance, successes or failures.

Instructions

If you haven't yet completed *Self-Talk: Finding a Positive Voice*, doing so first can enhance the effectiveness of this exercise.

1. Choose a specific situation to write about, that happened recently, or is ongoing in your life, that is creating stress or suffering for you. This exercise may initially stir up difficult emotions. Please choose a situation that is big enough to significantly impact your life, but not so big that you don't feel like you can handle it right now.

2. Bring mindful awareness to your experience, noticing your thoughts and feelings. Try to generate nonjudgmental acceptance, empathy and compassion for these difficult emotions, as you would for a friend.

3. Write yourself a letter, speaking as you would to a friend or loved one. Name all of your feelings and thoughts. You don't need to describe the event itself, just focus on identifying the thoughts and emotions you have about it.

_____

_____

_____

_____

_____

_____

_____

_____

Remind yourself that what you are going through is part of being human, and that many other people (known and unknown to you) have had similar experiences and emotions. Please bring these people to mind and write about your empathy for them, and how your shared experiences connect you.

_____

_____

_____

_____

_____

_____

_____

_____

_____

_____

_____

_____

_____

_____

_____

_____

_____

_____

_____

_____

4. Now, offer yourself kindness and guidance. You may choose to write from the perspective of a friend, your future self, or another positive voice. What words of encouragement, support, love and kindness can you offer? What strengths or resources can you point to that will help you get through this situation?

_____

_____

_____

_____

_____

_____

_____

_____

_____

_____

_____

_____

_____

_____

_____

_____

_____

_____

_____

_____

_____

_____

You can repeat this exercise anytime you are going through a difficult situation, or re-read this letter when you could use some self-compassion. More self-compassion exercises and meditations can be found at www. selfcompassion.org.

Please write a couple sentences about why you chose this activity. How do you think it might benefit you and others?

_____

_____

_____

_____

_____

How did it feel to write about this situation from a compassionate perspective?

_____

_____

_____

_____

How has this practice shifted your thoughts or feelings about this situation? (Don't worry if you haven't noticed any changes--the benefits may be immediate, or take place more gradually over time and with repetition of this exercise)

_____

_____

_____

_____

Is this a practice you'd like to continue? Why or why not?

_____

_____

_____

7
Check-in

Congratulations on completing week 2 of your ReST Workbook! Please take a moment to check-in with yourself about how you're doing, what you've learned, and where you want to go from here.

How are you doing this week?

_____

_____

_____

_____

_____

What have you noticed from week 2? Please describe anything you've learned, any progress you've made, or any changes you've noticed over the course of the week.

_____

_____

_____

_____

_____

What have you taken away that you would like to remember, or remind yourself of in the upcoming week?

_____

_____

_____

_____

_____

WEEK 3

Week 3
Menu of Activities

Please look through the descriptions of activities 1 through 6 on the following pages, choose which one(s) you would like to do this week, and write them down. You may choose 1 activity to do multiple times this week, or choose multiple activities to do once each. To get the most benefit, aim to practice some kind of wellness activity at least 3 times this week, in addition to the activities you are already practicing.

1. Set a Mini Goal

2. Emotional Skills: Give Yourself a Break

3. Social Connection: Really Listen

4. Health: Get in touch

5. Meaning: Explore/Affirm Your Beliefs

6. Self-Talk for Stressful Situations

7. Check-in

What activity/activities do you plan to do this week?

1. _____

2. _____

3. _____

When will you do them?

1. _____

2. _____

3. _____

1
Set a Mini Goal

This activity involves setting a small goal that can be accomplished within half an hour or less, that you can do today, or within the week.

Use when

You feel overwhelmed, or want a sense of accomplishment and competence.

Benefits [1,2]

- Helps generate movement and momentum

- Reduces inertia, anxiety and depression

- Provides a sense of control and accomplishment

- Prioritizes what is important to you

Why it Works

Setting goals prioritizes what is important to you, generates action, and engages your pre-frontal cortex, all of which work to reduce anxiety and depression. Because mini-goals are small, they are easy to achieve, and build your sense of competence and control. Accomplishing a goal triggers a burst of dopamine, which generates positive emotion and reinforces forward momentum.[3]

Instructions

Please identify one thing that you would like to do today, or within the week, that can be completed in 30 minutes or less. If you have a larger goal in mind, break it down into small steps and choose one to work on. Ideas for mini-goals include:

- Making time for a self-care activity

- Completing an item on your To Do list

- Connecting with someone you've lost touch with

- Tackling a minor task you've been procrastinating

- Doing something fun

Please describe your mini-goal:

_____

_____

_____

_____

What made you choose this particular goal? How do you think completing it might benefit yourself and others?

_____

_____

_____

_____

When will you do it?

_____

What might make it difficult to follow through on your mini goal?

_____

_____

_____

How will you overcome these obstacles?

_____

_____

_____

_____

_____

Notes. After you've done your mini-goal, take a moment to reflect on how it feels to have completed it.

_____

_____

_____

_____

_____

Is this a practice you'd like to continue? Why or why not?

_____

_____

_____

_____

_____

2

Emotional Skills: Give Yourself a Break

This practice involves taking breaks and engaging in self-care to replenish your energy and allow your mind and body to recover from stress.

Use When

you are stressed, overwhelmed or tired, and want to replenish your energy, renew your focus, and boost your productivity.

Benefits

Taking regular breaks and engaging in self-care:[4,5]

- Reduces stress, anxiety and fatigue

- Improves physical health and allows your body to recuperate from stress

- Improves focus, memory and learning

- Enhances efficiency and productivity

Why It Works

The human body is designed to alternate between spending and recovering energy, in roughly 90 minute cycles. Over this period of time, energy and focus become depleted. Strategic renewal, such as exercise, a change in scenery, a nap, or other forms of self-care will boost your productivity and performance and improve your health. Longer periods of rest, such as a fun weekend activity or vacation, are also essential to restoring energy and giving your mind time to rest.

Rather than trying to manage your time, it can be helpful to think about how to manage your energy. The practice of energy-management (periodic replenishment) will help you get more done, in less time, more sustainably.[4,5]

Instructions

Choose a self-care, or energy-replenishment strategy that you would like to practice this week. You may choose to take short breaks throughout the day, or engage in a longer period of self-care during the evening or on the weekend.

Please identify 5 self-care practices that you enjoy or would like to try:

1. _____

2. _____

3. _____

4. _____

5. _____

Please choose at least one that you would you like to try this week:

_____

When will you do it?

_____

What made you choose this particular goal? How do you think completing it might benefit you and others?

_____

_____

_____

_____

_____

What obstacles might make it difficult to follow through with engaging in self-care and taking breaks?

_____

_____

_____

_____

_____

How will you overcome these obstacles?

_____

_____

_____

_____

Notes. Once you've tried out your energy-replenishing strategy, take a moment to notice how it went. What was it like to do this activity? What impact did it have on you?

_____

_____

_____

_____

Is this a practice you'd like to continue? Why or why not?

_____

_____

_____

_____

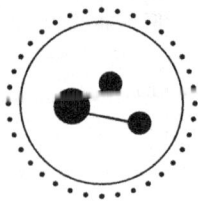

3
Social Connection: Really Listen

This practice involves giving someone your undivided attention, and really listening to how they are doing and what's on their mind.

Use When

You want to connect with others, make them feel good, and strengthen your relationships.

Benefits

This practice:[6,7,8]

- Deepens relationships and strengthens social ties

- Develops empathy and communication skills

- Improves well-being

Why It Works

Humans are social animals, and feeling socially connected is more strongly correlated with happiness than any other single factor.[9,10,11] The act of giving someone your full attention, and truly listening, helps you get to know that person, is a way to express caring, and gets your mirror neurons firing, which feeds empathy and connection. In this era of busyness, over-stimulation and distraction, giving someone your full attention is a rare gift.

Instructions

To engage in this simple, yet difficult practice, please focus on these areas as you interact with others:

- Be present and give your full attention to the other person, even if you only exchange a few words

- Practice trying to fully understand the other person's experience and perspective, rather than thinking about your own reactions, interpretations, or how to respond

- Express empathy, and validate their emotions rather than offering opinions or advice

What made you choose this practice? How do you think really listening might benefit you and others?

_____

_____

_____

_____

_____

When will you do it?

_____

What do you anticipate might make it difficult to be present, give your full attention, and really listen?

_____

_____

_____

_____

_____

How can you overcome these obstacles?

_____

_____

_____

_____

_____

Notes. Once you've practiced really listening, take a moment to notice how it went. How did you feel? How did the other person respond?

_____

_____

_____

_____

_____

Is this a practice you'd like to continue? Why or why not?

_____

_____

_____

_____

_____

4
Health: Get in Touch

This practice involves engaging in safe, healthy touch,
through massage, playing with pets, hugs,
or using self-comforting touch.

Use When

You want to soothe anxiety or stress, feel calmer and more relaxed, and connect with others.

Benefits

Touch has been shown to:[12,13]

- Calm fear, stress and anxiety

- Promote physical health

- Convey trust and connection

- Reduce pain

Why It Works

Basic warm touch, such as a pat on the back, touching the arm, or holding hands calms cardiovascular stress. It activates the body's vagus nerve, which is intimately involved with our compassionate response, and can trigger the release of oxytocin, which generates positive emotions and sense of connection. Touch can have some surprising benefits — one study showed that touching someone lightly on the upper arm increased tipping, as well as willingness to sign a petition or agree to a dance![12,13]

Instructions

Please choose how you would like to increase touch over the course of the week. Below are a few ideas, or you may choose your own. Please make sure the recipient is comfortable with hugs or touch.

- Schedule a massage

- Pet a pet! If you don't have a dog or cat of your own, you could volunteer at a shelter, or visit a friend's pet(s).

- Hug your partner, friends or family

- Practice lightly touching people on the arm during interactions with them

- Practice comforting yourself by stroking your arm or cheek, or resting your hand over your heart. People often think of touch as something we need from others, but your physiological response is the same whether you offer yourself soothing touch, or someone else does.[14]

What would you like to do to incorporate more touch in your week?

_____

_____

_____

_____

When and how will you do it?

_____

_____

_____

What made you choose this practice? How do you think it could benefit you and others?

_____

_____

_____

_____

What do you anticipate might make it difficult to engage in healthy touch?

_____

_____

_____

_____

How can you overcome these obstacles?

_____

_____

_____

_____

Notes. Once you've practiced healthy touch, take a moment to notice the impact it had. How did it feel to engage in more touch?

_____

_____

_____

_____

What changes, if any, did you notice in yourself or others?

_____

_____

_____

_____

Is this a practice you'd like to continue? Why or why not?

_____

_____

_____

_____

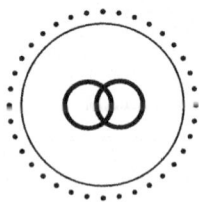

5
Meaning: *Explore/Affirm Your Beliefs*

This practice involves spending time reflecting on or reconnecting with what you believe in, whether these beliefs are secular, spiritual, or religious.

Use When

You want to feel calmer, connected to what's important to you, put difficulties into perspective, and improve your overall well-being.

Benefits

Believing in a benevolent power, being, or system beyond yourself, whether that is God, nature, a higher power, or something else, has been shown to:[9,10,15]

- Reduce stress, anxiety and depression

- Increase happiness

- Improve mental and physical health

Why It Works

There are several reasons why belief or faith in something beyond yourself works to improve mental and physical health and boost happiness:[9,10,12]

- The increased social connection and support of a religious or spiritual community

- An organizing set of positive beliefs to explain and make sense of the world (when people believe in a punitive or vengeful God, religion has a negative rather than positive impact on physical and mental health)

- The effects of meditation and prayer to regulate emotional responses, and over time train your brain to be calmer, and generate more positive emotion

- A set of principles that guides you to engage in healthy behaviors, such as not overindulging in substances, or treating others with compassion.

Instructions

There are many ways to explore or affirm your beliefs. You may pick from the options below, or choose something else that appeals to you.

- Attend a spiritual or religious service

- Talk to a friend, family member or spiritual/religious advisor about your beliefs, practices and values

- Write about your beliefs. You may respond to one or more of these questions, choose a topic of your own, or simply free write about what you believe in.

  - What do you think our purpose, or reason for being on earth, is?

  - Do you believe in a set of guiding principles, God, a higher power, or something else? Please describe what this means to you.

  - Do you believe we have a soul or spirit, and if so, what does that mean to you?

I believe...

_____

_____

_____

_____

_____

_____

_____

_____

_____

_____

_____

_____

_____

_____

_____

_____

_____

_____

_____

_____

_____

_____

_____

_____

Please write a couple of sentences about why you've chosen this activity. How do you think it might benefit yourself and others?

_____

_____

_____

How can you stay connected to your beliefs, especially during times of stress?

What obstacles might come up to make it difficult to do this?

_____

_____

_____

What can you do to overcome these obstacles?

_____

_____

_____

Once you've completed this practice, please take a moment to reflect on how it went. How did it feel to explore or affirm your beliefs? What impact, if any, did you notice?

_____

_____

_____

_____

Is this a practice you'd like to continue? Why or why not?

_____

_____

_____

6
Self-Talk for Stressful Situations

This activity involves recognizing the positive aspects of your stress response and engaging in positive self-talk in stressful situations.

Use When

You are facing a challenging situation that triggers your stress response, such as an exam or presentation, public performance, interview, competition, difficult conversation, etc.

Benefits

Acknowledging the positive aspects of stress:[11,23,24,25]

- Builds confidence and improves performance

- Helps you recover from stress more quickly

- Buffers against the negative mental and physical effects of stress

Why it Works

What you tell yourself about stressful events shapes how you feel about them, how you respond in challenging moments, and how quickly you recover from difficulties. The simple act of changing your story about stress can make a big difference to your emotional experience, and help you bring your best self to challenges. Research has shown that stress actually *improves* performance, as long as you're not stressed about it! [11,23,24,25]

Instructions

- When you notice the first sign of "nerves" (increased heart rate and breathing, butterflies in the stomach), say to yourself, "I'm excited!" "I'm pumped!" "I'm psyched!" or your own words to that effect. The states of anxiety and excitement are physiologically very similar, which makes reframing nerves as excitement far more effective than trying to calm down, which is the physiological opposite of elevated stress.

- Remind yourself that the stress is actually helping you do well by giving you extra energy and focus by preparing you to rise to the challenge. Then focus on channeling the energy into the task at hand.

- Tell yourself, "You've got this! You can do this!" and remind yourself that this challenge is making you stronger and more capable, and is preparing you to meet future challenges.

Please write a couple sentences about why you've chosen this activity. How do you think it might benefit you and others?

_____

_____

_____

_____

How will you remember to engage in positive self-talk during times of stress?

_____

_____

_____

What obstacles might come up to make it difficult to do this?

_____

_____

_____

_____

What can you do to overcome these obstacles?

_____

_____

_____

Once you've practiced positive self-talk in a stressful situation, please take a moment to reflect on how it went. How did it feel to talk to yourself in this way?

_____

_____

_____

_____

What impact did it have on how you felt and how you handled the situation?

_____

_____

_____

_____

Is this a practice you'd like to continue? Why or why not?

_____

_____

_____

_____

7
Check-in

Congratulations on completing the third week of your ReST Workbook! Please take a moment to check-in with yourself about how you're doing, what you've learned, and where you want to go from here.

How are you doing this week?

_____

_____

_____

_____

What have you noticed from week 3? Please describe anything you've learned, any progress you've made, or any changes you've noticed over the course of the week.

_____

_____

_____

_____

What have you taken away that you would like to remember, or remind yourself of in the upcoming week?

_____

_____

_____

WEEK 4

Week 4
Menu of Activities

Please look through the activities, choose which one(s) you would like to do this week, and write them down. You may choose 1 activity to do multiple times this week, or choose multiple activities to do once each. To get the most benefit, aim to practice some kind of wellness activity at least 3 times this week, in addition to what you already do.

1. Set a Mini Goal

2. Emotional Skills: Watch Your Mental Diet

3. Social Connection: Express Appreciation

4. Health: Breathe

5. Meaning: Benefit-Finding

6. Self-Talk: Create an Effective Affirmation

7. Check-in

What activity/activities do you plan to do this week?

1. _____

2. _____

3. _____

When will you do them?

1. _____

2. _____

3. _____

1
Set a Mini Goal

This activity involves setting a small goal that can be accomplished within half an hour or less, that you can do today, or within the week.

Use when

You feel overwhelmed, or want a sense of accomplishment and competence.

Benefits [1,2]

- Helps generate movement and momentum

- Reduces inertia, anxiety and depression

- Provides a sense of control and accomplishment

- Prioritizes what is important to you

Why it Works

Setting goals prioritizes what is important to you, generates action, and engages your pre-frontal cortex, all of which work to reduce anxiety and depression. Because mini-goals are small, they are easy to achieve, and build your sense of competence and control. Accomplishing a goal triggers a burst dopamine, which generates positive emotion and reinforces forward momentum.[3]

Instructions

Please identify one thing that you would like to do today, or within the week, that can be completed in 30 minutes or less. If you have a larger goal in mind, break it down into small steps and choose one to work on. Ideas for mini-goals include:

- Making time for a self-care activity

- Completing an item on your To Do list

- Connecting with someone you've lost touch with

- Tackling a minor task you've been procrastinating

- Doing something fun

Please describe your mini-goal:

_____

_____

_____

_____

_____

What made you choose this particular goal? How do you think completing it might benefit yourself and others?

_____

_____

_____

_____

_____

When will you do it?

_____

What might make it difficult to follow through on your mini goal?

_____

_____

_____

_____

_____

How will you overcome these obstacles?

_____

_____

_____

_____

_____

Notes. After you've done your mini-goal, take a moment to reflect on how it feels to have completed it.

_____

_____

_____

_____

_____

Is this a practice you'd like to continue? Why or why not?

_____

_____

_____

_____

_____

2

Emotional Skills: Watch Your Mental Diet

This practice involves being mindful of your media use, and whether it is helpful or harmful to your mood and well-being.

Use When

You want to reduce anxiety, and increase calm, hope and connection.

Benefits

Research has shown that limiting your use of social media, pornography, and talk shows can:[4,5,6]

- Reduce depression and anxiety, and improve mood

- Foster deeper, more genuine social connections

- Reclaim time to engage in what is important to you

- Improve sleep

Why It Works

Nonfictional media can trick you into believing that what is shown is representative of reality. Social media tends to draw your attention to the highlights of your friends' lives, and obscure the hardships. Use of Facebook has been shown to contribute to depression by inviting negative social comparison (they're happier, more successful and having more fun than you) and FOMO (fear of missing out – you're not included in the fun they're having).[4,6] The news draws your attention in the opposite direction, to disasters and violence, which can skew your perception of the frequency of these events, and has been shown to predict fear, anxiety and distrust.[5]

Instructions

Take a moment to reflect back on your media use over the past week. Please make a list of the media you used on a typical day this week, including surfing the web, the programs you watch or listen to, social media, what you read, and the music you listen to.

List of a typical day of media use:

_____

_____

_____

How much time do you spend using media, on a typical day?

_____

How do you feel about your media use, and what impact do you think it has on you?

_____

_____

_____

_____

Please choose 1 day in the upcoming week to practice mindful media use. Throughout the day, notice how you feel before, during and after using particular types of media.

Schedule your Mindful Media Day

_____

After you've completed this practice, please write about what you noticed. What did you learn about how particular types of media make you feel?

_____

_____

_____

_____

Based on this practice, what changes, if any, would you like to make to your use of media?

_____

_____

_____

_____

What made you choose this goal? What benefits do you think this could have on you or others?

_____

_____

_____

_____

What obstacles might make it difficult to follow through with this goal?

_____

_____

_____

_____

What can you do to overcome these obstacles?

_____

_____

_____

_____

3

Social Connection: *Express Appreciation*

This practice involves expressing gratitude and
appreciation for others.

Use When

You want to improve your relationships and lift someone else's mood as
well as your own.

Benefits

Taking a few minutes to express appreciation:[7-11]

- Gives you and the recipient a major mood boost

- Strengthens relationships

Why It Works

Focusing on your relationships may be the best investment you can
make in your health and well-being, and expressing appreciation may be
the single most powerful approach to improving relationships.[7-11]
Research has found that strong, healthy relationships rely on a ratio of at
least 5 positive interactions and communications to every negative
one.[11] Everyone wants to be appreciated, so verbalizing what you value
about someone will give them a boost, bring you closer together, and
may even lead to reciprocation. This practice also helps you train your
brain to notice the positive, counteracting the brain's natural tendency to
focus on flaws and irritants.[9]

Instructions

There are a number of ways you can express appreciation, including:

- Tell someone how they have had a positive impact on you or made a difference in your life

- Tell someone what you like, respect and admire about them

- Thank people for their contributions

- Give a great compliment

Please be specific about exactly what you appreciate and why. For example, "Thank you for _____. It means a lot to me because _____" or, "I think you're awesome because of _____, _____ and _____."

Please describe how you would like to carry out appreciation practice. Is there a particular person you would like to express appreciation to? Or would you prefer to practice expressing appreciation to the people you interact with throughout the day? Or something else?

_____

_____

_____

_____

If you like, you can jot down some thoughts, or create a rough draft of what you'd like to share here: Who do you appreciate, and what do you appreciate about them?

_____

_____

_____

_____

_____

_____

ReST: The Resiliency Skills Training Workbook

What made you choose to do this practice? How do you think it might benefit yourself and others?

_____

_____

_____

When will you do it?

_____

What obstacles might get in the way of expressing appreciation?

_____

_____

_____

_____

How will you overcome these obstacles?

_____

_____

_____

Notes: Once you've completed this practice, take a moment to reflect on what you noticed. How did this practice make you feel? How did the recipient(s) of your appreciation respond?

_____

_____

_____

_____

Is this a practice you'd like to continue? Why or why not?

_____

_____

_____

4
Health: Breathe

This activity involves regularly practicing deep, slow breathing.

Use When

You are stressed or anxious, or want to relax and improve your energy.

Benefits

Deep breathing has been shown to: [12]

- Increase relaxation and calm

- Decrease stress, tension and anxiety

- Improve mental and physical functioning

Why It Works

Deep breathing improves oxygen delivery to your brain and body, which enhances mental focus and physical energy. It improves physical health by relaxing muscle tension, reducing blood pressure, and removing toxins more efficiently. Deep breathing also triggers the release of endorphins, which generate feelings of contentment and relieve pain.[12]

Instructions

You may choose to explore the multitude of breathing exercises available online, or use the simple practice outlined below. Try to tune into your breath several times throughout the day, and practice deep breathing for a couple minutes each time.

1. Become mindful of your breath, and your current breathing pattern.

2. If you are able, start breathing through your nose and into your belly. It may be helpful to put one hand on your belly and one on your chest, to help you direct your breath.

3. Begin to slowly count during your inhalations and exhalations. Aim to extend your inhalation for a count of 4 and your exhalation for a count of 4. Do not push yourself if this is uncomfortable - your breath will gradually slow down over time, with practice.

4. Now focus on making your breath smooth, so the transition from the inhale flows smoothly into the exhale and vice versa.

What made you choose to do this practice? How do you think it might benefit you and others?

_____

_____

_____

How will you remember to practice deep breathing?

_____

_____

After: Once you've completed deep breathing practice a few times, take a moment to reflect on what you noticed. How do you feel practicing deep breathing? What impact, if any, has it had on you?

_____

_____

_____

Is this a practice you'd like to continue? Why or why not?

_____

_____

_____

5

Meaning: Benefit-Finding

This practice involves writing about the learning, growth or other positive outcomes that can arise from a stressful, painful or negative event.

Use When

A specific situation or event is having a negative impact on your life, and you would like to let go of resentment, anger, shame, hurt, or other painful emotions, and move forward.

Benefits

Finding the positive aspects of stressful or negative events has been shown to:[6,13]

- Improve physical health

- Reduce stress and depression

- Build confidence

- Strengthen relationships

Why It Works

Even when bad things happen, the meaning that you make out of the experience strongly influences your recovery and how you respond. Benefit-finding practice is not meant to minimize difficult events or painful emotions. Instead, it helps widen your perspective to include both the negative and positive outcomes from these events. It can also empower you and give you a sense of control over how you choose to move forward. This sense of control is a key predictor of resiliency and positive growth.[6,12]

Instructions

To get the most out of this practice, please choose an experience that has affected you deeply, rather than a minor stressor, and write in freely for 10-15 minutes in response to the prompts below. You may find it helpful to write about the same situation for several consecutive days.

Please choose an experience or ongoing situation in your life that is causing you stress. Write about your feelings and the impact this event or situation has had on you, both positive and negative.

_____

_____

_____

_____

_____

_____

_____

_____

_____

_____

_____

_____

_____

_____

_____

_____

_____

_____

_____

_____

_____

_____

What benefits have you experienced as a result of this experience? In what ways is your life better because of it? Have you changed in any positive way as a result of coping with this experience? (Please remember that *you*, not the negative event, deserve the sole credit for any positive outcomes or changes you make).

_____

_____

_____

_____

_____

_____

_____

_____

_____

_____

_____

_____

_____

_____

_____

_____

_____

_____

_____

_____

_____

_____

_____

What made you choose this practice? How do you think it might benefit you and others?

_____

_____

_____

_____

_____

Notes: Once you've completed this practice, take a moment to reflect on what you noticed. How did it feel to reflect on this situation, and actively seek out benefits that came out of the situation and how you handled it?

_____

_____

_____

_____

_____

Is this a practice you'd like to continue? Why or why not?

_____

_____

_____

_____

_____

6
Self-Talk: *Create an Effective Affirmation*

This practice involves creating a personal affirmation (a sentence or mantra) to say or repeat to yourself to encourage positive growth.

Use When

You want to quiet your self-critical voice, improve how you see and treat yourself, or motivate yourself to tackle a goal or challenge.

Benefits

An effective affirmation:[14,15,16]

- Improves your self-image, mood and well-being

- Motivates and encourages you to persist through challenges and accomplish important goals

Why It Works

How you talk to yourself has an enormous impact on your mood and behavior. A self-critical voice can make you afraid to take risks or pursue challenging goals because the inevitable setbacks and mistakes along the way invite harsh judgement. This style of self-talk contributes to depression and anxiety, whereas compassionate, supportive and encouraging self-talk contributes to successful goal-achievement and positive mood. Affirmations that focus on your values or behavioral ideals can shape your actions by serving as a reminder of the kind of person you want to be.[14,15,16]

Instructions

It is important to word an affirmation carefully, because repeating affirmations that you don't actually believe can make you feel *worse*. For example, if you tell yourself you are confident, beautiful and successful, when you *feel* the exact opposite, the affirmation may simply highlight the gap between your experience and your ideal. This is why compliments often don't sink in, or change your opinion of yourself. To create an effective affirmation:

1. Choose an area you would like to focus on, such as a goal that you'd like to motivate yourself to keep moving toward. Please write about what you would like to achieve with the affirmation.

   _____

   _____

   _____

2. Identify a compassionate, encouraging perspective. We aren't always our best cheerleaders, so it can help to use the voice of a friend, mentor, superhero, future self, etc. (The "Find a Positive Voice" exercise on page 26 will help you do this).

3. Create a short, one-sentence affirmation that:

   a. Is honest and rings true to you

   b. Focuses on your values, strengths and abilities

   c. Places emphasis on behavior that you have control over, rather than fixed traits

   d. Feels supportive or motivating

For example, an effective affirmation could be, "You are courageous and hard-working" or "You are kind and generous" which describe behaviors we are able to change at will. You can adapt your affirmation at any time to target what you need in a given moment.

_____

_____

_____

What made you choose to do this practice? How do you think it might benefit yourself and others?

_____

_____

_____

_____

_____

How will you remember to use your affirmation?

_____

_____

_____

_____

Notes: Once you've practiced using your affirmation, a few times, take a moment to reflect on what you notice. How does it feel to practice your affirmation? What impact, if any, has it had on you?

_____

_____

_____

_____

Is this a practice you'd like to continue? Why or why not?

_____

_____

_____

_____

7
Check-in

Congratulations on completing the fourth and final week of your ReST Workbook! Please take a moment to check-in with yourself about how you're doing, what you've learned, and where you want to go from here.

How are you doing this week?

_____

_____

_____

_____

What have you noticed since starting the workbook? Please describe what you've learned, the progress you've made, or any changes you've noticed over the course of the month.

_____

_____

_____

_____

What have you taken away that you would like to remember, or remind yourself of in the future?

_____

_____

_____

ASSESS YOUR PROGRESS!

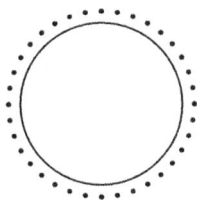

Assess Your Progress!

If you'd like, you can take a moment to assess any progress you've made in the areas you identified at the start of the workbook. Please copy the questions, or areas you wanted to assess, as you wrote them.

1. Please write the first question, or area you chose to assess, here:

_____

_____

_____

Please circle where you fall in this area now, averaging over the past 2 weeks. Use a scale of 1-10, with 1 being the lowest possible and 10 being the highest possible.

1   2   3   4   5   6   7   8   9   10

2. Please write the second question, or area you chose to assess, here:

_____

_____

_____

Please circle where you fall in this area now, averaging over the past 2 weeks. Use a scale of 1-10, with 1 being the lowest possible and 10 being the highest possible.

1   2   3   4   5   6   7   8   9   10

3. If applicable, please write the third question, or area you chose to assess, here:

_____

_____

_____

Please circle where you fall in this area now, averaging over the past 2 weeks. Use a scale of 1-10, with 1 being the lowest possible and 10 being the highest possible.

1   2   3   4   5   6   7   8   9   10

I hope you have enjoyed The Resiliency Skills Training Workbook.

Weekly charts are included on the following pages to track the exercises you have tried and how you like them. There are also a number of blank note pages in case you would like to repeat any of the exercises, or make notes.

If you have found this workbook helpful, please consider writing a review on Amazon. Feel free to email me directly about your experiences using the exercises—I would love to hear from you! If you are interested in using *The Resiliency Skills Training Workbook* in a group, training, or online wellness program, you may download a free facilitator's manual from my website.

I wish you all the best in your journey.

Sincerely,
Jessica Gifford
Founder, Well Student

jessica@wellstudent.co
https://wellstudent.co

Scan code to leave a review on Amazon, thanks!

TRACK YOUR ACTIVITIES!

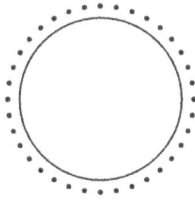

Track Your Activities!

This chart will enable you to keep a record of the activities you've tried and whether or not you found them helpful and enjoyable. You may find some exercises beneficial, but difficult to incorporate into your routine or lifestyle (poor fit), while others may be fun but less impactful. Taking notes after you've completed each activity will help you remember which activities worked best for you. If you like, you can create a rating scale to capture impact and fit, or simply jot down your thoughts. If you would like to turn an activity into a habit, it will be easier to do so with one that you enjoy or notice benefits from. Please be aware that some activities have a subtle impact over time, and with repetition.

Week 1 Activities

Activity	# Of Times Practiced (Tally)	Impact/Benefit	Enjoyment/Fit
1. Mini Goal:			
2. Emotional Skills: Noting Practice			
3. Social Connection: Smile!			
4. Health: Improve Your Sleep			
5. Meaning: Spend Time in Nature			
6. Self-Talk: Find a Positive Voice			

Notes

Week 2 Activities

Activity	# Of Times Practiced (Tally)	Impact/Benefit	Enjoyment/Fit
1. Mini Goal:			
2. Emotional Skills: What Went Well and Why			
3. Social Connection: Acts of Kindness			
4. Health: Exercise			
5. Meaning: Explore Your Values			
6. Self-Talk: Write Yourself A Letter			

Notes

Week 3 Activities

Activity	# Of Times Practiced (Tally)	Impact/Benefit	Enjoyment/Fit
1. Mini Goal:			
2. Emotional Skills: Give Yourself A Break			
3. Social Connection: Really Listen			
4. Health: Get In Touch			
5. Meaning: Explore/Affirm Your Beliefs			
6. Self-Talk for Stressful Situations			

Notes

Week 4 Activities

Activity	# Of Times Practiced (Tally)	Impact/Benefit	Enjoyment/Fit
1. Mini Goal:			
2. Emotional Skills: Watch Your Mental Diet			
3. Social Connection: Express Appreciation			
4. Health: Breathe			
5. Meaning: Benefit-Finding			
6. Self-Talk: Create an Effective Affirmation			

Notes

Notes

_____

_____

_____

_____

_____

_____

_____

_____

_____

_____

_____

_____

_____

_____

_____

_____

_____

_____

_____

_____

_____

_____

_____

_____

_____

Notes

Notes

_____

_____

_____

_____

_____

_____

_____

_____

_____

_____

_____

_____

_____

_____

_____

_____

_____

_____

_____

_____

_____

_____

_____

_____

Notes

Notes

ReST: The Resiliency Skills Training Workbook

Notes

Acknowledgements

I am incredibly grateful for the rapidly expanding field of research that focuses on promoting health and expanding human potential, rather than on managing illness. A profound thank you to the many researchers and authors who have identified, developed, and evolved concrete, evidence-based strategies to support thriving. Your work is the foundation of this book.

Writing, creating, and putting my work out in the world has stretched me in new ways. The process has been alternately exciting, tedious, rewarding, and scary. I am incredibly grateful to my wife Nicole, who has been unflaggingly supportive in the face of this emotional roller coaster! Nicole, thank you for always believing in me – it means more than I can possibly express. My brother and graphic designer extraordinaire, Isaiah King, transformed a pile of words into a neatly organized, visually appealing workbook, and remained patient through multiple edits and revisions – thank you! To the friends, family and colleagues who offered feedback and words of support and encouragement, I could not have done this without you.

Endnotes

INTRODUCTION

1. Oettingen, G. (2014). *Rethinking positive thinking: Inside the new science of motivation.* New York: Current.

2. Patterson, K. (2011). *Change anything: The new science of personal success.* New York: Business Plus.

3. Medina, J. (2008). *Brain rules: 12 principles for surviving and thriving at work, home, and school.* Seattle, WA: Pear Press.

4. Dweck, C. S. (2006). *Mindset: The new psychology of success.* New York: Random House.

5. Hanson, R. (2015). *Hardwiring Happiness.* Random House USA.

6. Crocker, J., Olivier, M., & Nuer, N. (2009). Self-image Goals and Compassionate Goals: Costs and Benefits. *Self and Identity,* 8(2-3), 251-269. doi:10.1080/15298860802505160

7. Yeager, D. S., Henderson, M. D., Paunesku, D., Walton, G. M., D'mello, S., Spitzer, B. J., & Duckworth, A. L. (2014). Boring but important: A self-transcendent purpose for learning fosters academic self-regulation. *Journal of Personality and Social Psychology,* 107(4), 559-580.

8. McGonigal, K. (2015). *The upside of stress: Why stress is good for you, and how to get good at it.* New York: Penguin Random House.

WEEK 1

1. Amabile, T., & Kramer, S. (2011). *The progress principle: Using small wins to ignite joy, engagement, and creativity at work.* Boston, MA: Harvard Business Review Press.

2. Patterson, K. (2011). *Change anything: The new science of personal success.* New York: Business Plus.

3. Korb, A. (2016). *The upward spiral: using neuroscience to reverse the course of depression, one small change at a time.* Strawberry Hills, NSW: ReadHowYouWant.

4. Kay, K. S. (2014). *The Confidence Code: The science and art of self-assurance—what women should know.* New York: HarperCollins.

5. Harris, R. (2011). *The Confidence Gap: A guide to overcoming fear and self-doubt.* Boston: Trumpeter.

6. Goulston, M., & Ferrazzi, K. (2010). *Just Listen*. New York, NY: AMACOM.

7. McGonigal, K. (2012). *The willpower instinct: How self-control works, why it matters, and what you can do to get more of it*. New York: Avery.

8. Neff, K. (2011) *Self-Compassion: The Proven Power of Being Kind to Yourself*. New York: HarperCollins.

9. Rubin, G. (2009). *The happiness project: Or why I spent a year trying to sing in the morning, clean my closets, fight right, read Aristotle, and generally have more fun*. New York, NY: Harper.

10. Huffington, A. S. (2016). *The sleep revolution: Transforming your life, one night at a time*.

11. Medina, J. (2008). *Brain rules: 12 principles for surviving and thriving at work, home, and school*. Seattle, WA: Pear Press.

12. Publications, H. H. (2009, July). Sleep and mental health. Retrieved April 09, 2017, from http://www.health.harvard.edu/newsletter_article/Sleep-and-mental-health

13. Segovia, F., Moore, J. L., Linnville, S., Hoyt, R. E., & Hain, R. E. (2013). Sleep and Resilience: A Longitudinal 37-Year Follow-up Study of Vietnam Repatriated Prisoners of War. *Military Medicine, 178*(2), 196-201. doi:10.7205/milmed-d-12-00227

14. This Is Your Brain on Nature. (2017, February 22). Retrieved February 26, 2017, from http://www.nationalgeographic.com/magazine/2016/01/call-to-wild/

15. Bratman, G. N., Hamilton, J. P., Hahn, K. S., Daily, G. C., & Gross, J. J. (2015). Nature experience reduces rumination and subgenual prefrontal cortex activation. *Proceedings of the National Academy of Sciences, 112*(28), 8567-8572. doi:10.1073/pnas.1510459112

16. Lauren F Friedman and Kevin Loria. (2014, April 09). 11 Scientifically Proven Reasons You Should Go Outside. Retrieved February 26, 2017, from http://www.businessinsider.com/11-reasons-you-should-go-outside-2014-4

17. Jensen, P. (2006). A Potential Natural Treatment for Attention-Deficit/Hyperactivity Disorder: Evidence From a National Study. *Yearbook of Psychiatry and Applied Mental Health, 2006*, 53-54. doi:10.1016/s0084-3970(08)70057-4

18. Park, B. J., Tsunetsugu, Y., Kasetani, T., Kagawa, T., & Miyazaki, Y. (2009). The physiological effects of Shinrin-yoku (taking in the forest atmosphere or forest bathing): evidence from field experiments in 24 forests across Japan. *Environmental Health and Preventive Medicine, 15*(1), 18-26. doi:10.1007/s12199-009-0086-9

19. Mitchell, R. J., Richardson, E. A., Shortt, N. K., & Pearce, J. R. (2015). Neighborhood Environments and Socioeconomic Inequalities in Mental Well-Being. *American Journal of Preventive Medicine,* 49(1), 80-84. doi:10.1016/j.amepre.2015.01.017

20. Mehl-Madrona, L. (2010). *Healing the mind through the power of story: the promise of narrative psychiatry.* Rochester, VT: Bear & Company.

WEEK 2

1. Amabile, T., & Kramer, S. (2011). *The progress principle: Using small wins to ignite joy, engagement, and creativity at work.* Boston, MA: Harvard Business Review Press.

2. Patterson, K. (2011). *Change anything: The new science of personal success.* New York: Business Plus.

3. Korb, A. (2016). *The upward spiral: using neuroscience to reverse the course of depression, one small change at a time.* Strawberry Hills, NSW: ReadHowYouWant.

4. Seligman, M. E. (2011) *Flourish: A Visionary New Understanding of Happiness and Well-being.* New York: Free Press.

5. Seligman, M. E., Steen, T. A., Park, N., & Peterson, C. (2005). Positive Psychology Progress: Empirical Validation of Interventions. *American Psychologist,* 60(5), 410-421. doi:10.1037/0003-066x.60.5.410

6. Emmons, R. A. (2007). *Thanks!: How the new science of gratitude can make you happier.* Boston: Houghton Mifflin.

7. Lyubomirsky, S. (2008). *The how of happiness: A scientific approach to getting the life you want.* New York: Penguin Press.

8. Seligman, M. E. (2002). *Authentic happiness: Using the new positive psychology to realize your potential for lasting fulfillment.* New York: Free Press.

9. Achor, S. (2013). *Before happiness: The 5 hidden keys to achieving success, spreading happiness, and sustaining positive change.* New York: Crown Business.

10. Keyes, C. L., & Haidt, J. (2003). *Flourishing: Positive psychology and the life well-lived.* Washington, DC: American Psychological Association.

11. McGonigal, K. (2015). *The upside of stress: Why stress is good for you, and how to get good at it.* New York: Penguin Random House.

12. Medina, J. (2008). *Brain rules: 12 principles for surviving and thriving at work, home, and school.* Seattle, WA: Pear Press.

13. Levine, J. A. (2014) *Get up!: why your chair is killing you and what you can do about it.* New York, NY: Palgrave Macmillan.

14. Carek, P. J., Laibstain, S. E., & Carek, S. M. (n.d.). Exercise for the treatment of depression and anxiety. Retrieved July 27, 2017, from https://www.ncbi.nlm.nih.gov/pubmed/21495519

15. Lee, D., Pate, R. R., Lavie, C. J., Sui, X., Church, T. S., & Blair, S. N. (2014). Leisure-Time Running Reduces All-Cause and Cardiovascular Mortality Risk. *Journal of the American College of Cardiology, 64*(5), 472-481. doi:10.1016/j.jacc.2014.04.058

16. Buettner, D. (2010). *The blue zones: lessons for living longer from the people who've lived the longest.* Washington, D.C.: National Geographic Society.

17. Duckworth, A. (2016) *Grit: The power of passion and perseverance.* New York: Scribner.

18. Sinek, S. (2013). *Start with why: how great leaders inspire everyone to take action.* London: Portfolio/Penguin.

19. Miller, W. R., & Rollnick, S. (1992). *Motivational interviewing: preparing people to change.* New York, NY: The Guilford Press.

20. Neff, K. (2011) *Self-Compassion: The Proven Power of Being Kind to Yourself.* New York: HarperCollins.

21. McGonigal, K. (2012). *The willpower instinct: How self-control works, why it matters, and what you can do to get more of it.* New York: Avery.

22. Seligman, M. E. (2011). *Learned optimism.* North Sydney, N.S.W.: Random House Australia.

23. McGonigal, K. (n.d.). How to make stress your friend. Retrieved February 27, 2017, from https://www.ted.com/talks/kelly_mcgonigal_how_to_make_stress_your_friend

24. Brooks, A. W. (2014). Get excited: Reappraising pre-performance anxiety as excitement. Journal of Experimental Psychology: General, 143(3), 1144-1158. doi:10.1037/a0035325

25. Jamieson, J. P., Mendes, W. B., Blackstock, E., & Schmader, T. (2010). Turning the knots in your stomach into bows: Reappraising arousal improves performance on the GRE. *Journal of Experimental Social Psychology, 46*(1), 208-212. doi:10.1016/j.jesp.2009.08.015

WEEK 3

1. Amabile, T., & Kramer, S. (2011). *The progress principle: Using small wins to ignite joy, engagement, and creativity at work.* Boston, MA: Harvard Business Review Press.

2. Patterson, K. (2011). *Change anything: The new science of personal success.* New York: Business Plus.

3. Korb, A. (2016). *The upward spiral: using neuroscience to reverse the course of depression, one small change at a time.* Strawberry Hills, NSW: ReadHowYouWant.

4. Schwartz, T. (2013, February 09). Opinion | Relax! You'll Be More Productive. Retrieved December 18, 2017, from http://www.nytimes.com/2013/02/10/opinion/sunday/relax-youll-be-more-productive.html

5. McCarthy, T. S., William Oncken, Jr. and Donald L. Wass, Ghoshal, H. B., & Mankins, M. C. (2015, July 16). Manage Your Energy, Not Your Time. Retrieved December 18, 2017, from https://hbr.org/2007/10/manage-your-energy-not-your-time

6. Ornish, D. (1999) *Love and Survival: 8 Pathways to Intimacy and Health.* New York: Harper Perennial.

7. Brown, B. (2012). *Daring greatly: How the courage to be vulnerable transforms the way we live, love, parent, and lead.* New York, NY: Gotham Books.

8. Goulston, M. (2010). *Just Listen: Discover the Secret to Getting Through to Absolutely Anyone.* New York: AMACOM.

9. Lyubomirsky, S. (2008). *The how of happiness: A scientific approach to getting the life you want.* New York: Penguin Press.

10. Seligman, M. E. (2002). *Authentic happiness: Using the new positive psychology to realize your potential for lasting fulfillment.* New York: Free Press.

11. Keyes, C. L., & Haidt, J. (2003). *Flourishing: Positive psychology and the life well-lived.* Washington, DC: American Psychological Association.

12. Hands On Research: The Science of Touch. (n.d.). Retrieved December 18, 2017, from https://greatergood.berkeley.edu/article/item/hands_on_research

13. Wiseman, R. (2015). *59 seconds: think a little, change a lot.* London: Pan Books.

14. Neff, K. (2011) *Self-Compassion: The Proven Power of Being Kind to Yourself.* New York: HarperCollins.

15. Rettner, R. (2015, September 23) God Help Us? How Religion is Good (And Bad) For Mental Health. Retrieved December 18, 2017, from https://www.livescience.com/52197-religion-mental-health-brain.html

WEEK 4

1. Amabile, T., & Kramer, S. (2011). *The progress principle: Using small wins to ignite joy, engagement, and creativity at work.* Boston, MA: Harvard Business Review Press.

2. Patterson, K. (2011). *Change anything: The new science of personal success.* New York: Business Plus.

3. Korb, A. (2016). *The upward spiral: using neuroscience to reverse the course of depression, one small change at a time.* Strawberry Hills, NSW: ReadHowYouWant.

4. Walton, A. G. (2017, October 03). 6 Ways Social Media Affects Our Mental Health. Retrieved December 18, 2017, from https://www.forbes.com/sites/alicegwalton/2017/06/30/a-run-down-of-social-medias-effects-on-our-mental-health/

5. Lustig, R. H. (2017). *The hacking of the American mind: inside the sugar-coated plot to confuse pleasure with happiness.* New York: Avery.

6. McGonigal, K. (2015). *The upside of stress: Why stress is good for you, and how to get good at it.* New York: Penguin Random House.

7. Achor, S. (2011). *The happiness advantage: the seven principles that fuel success and performance at work.* London: Virgin.

8. Keyes, C. L., & Haidt, J. (2003). *Flourishing: Positive psychology and the life well-lived.* Washington, DC: American Psychological Association.

9. Seligman, M. E. (2002). *Authentic happiness: Using the new positive psychology to realize your potential for lasting fulfillment.* New York: Free Press.

10. Emmons, R. A. (2007). *Thanks!: How the new science of gratitude can make you happier.* Boston: Houghton Mifflin.

11. Gottman, J., & Silver, N. (1994). *Why marriages succeed or fail and how you can make yours last.* New York: Fireside.

12. Publishing, H. H. (n.d.). Relaxation techniques: Breath control helps quell errant stress response. Retrieved December 18, 2017, from https://www.health.harvard.edu/mind-and-mood/relaxation-techniques-breath-control-helps-quell-errant-stress-response

13. Seligman, M. E. (2011) *Flourish: A Visionary New Understanding of Happiness and Well-being.* New York: Free Press.

14. Dweck, C. S. (2006). Mindset: *The new psychology of success.* New York: Random House.

15. Mehl-Madrona, L. (2010). *Healing the mind through the power of story: the promise of narrative psychiatry.* Rochester, VT: Bear & Company.

16. Neff, K. (2011) *Self-Compassion: The Proven Power of Being Kind to Yourself.* New York: HarperCollins.